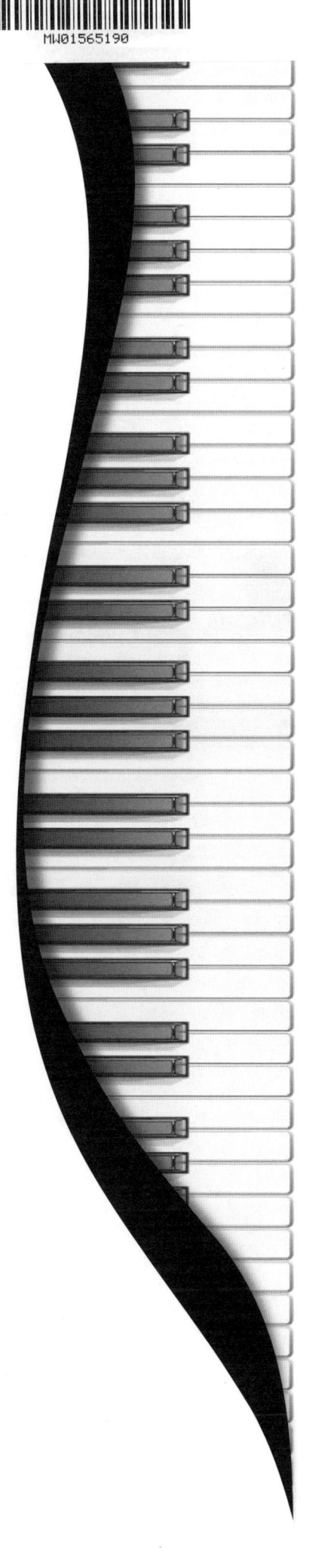

Songs I Love to Play!
VOLUME TWO

19 Motivating Solos for Late Beginners

Music by
Jennifer Eklund

PIANO PRONTO PUBLISHING

PianoPronto.com

Songs I Love to Play! Volume Two

Jennifer Eklund

Edited by Meagan Mason & Hannah Winebarger

Copyright © 2013 Piano Pronto Publishing, Inc.
All Rights Reserved.

WARNING: The compositions, arrangements, text, and graphics in this publication are protected by copyright law. No part of this work may be duplicated or reprinted without the prior consent of the author.

ISBN 978-0-9886406-8-9

Printed in the United States of America

Piano Pronto Publishing
PianoPronto.com

Songs I Love to Play!
VOLUME TWO

ABOVE & BEYOND 1

THE STARS & STRIPES FOREVER 3

IN THE HALL OF THE MOUNTAIN KING 5

YOU'RE A GRAND OLD FLAG 7

RONDALLA ARAGONESA 9

TAKE ME OUT TO THE BALL GAME 11

CANON 13

HUNGARIAN RHAPSODY 15

JE TE VEUX 17

NON PIÙ ANDRAI 19

THE RETURN 21

PINEAPPLE RAG 23

WHIRLWIND 26

LÀ CI DAREM LA MANO 29

TURKISH MARCH 32

MAPLE LEAF RAG 35

THURSDAY BLUES 39

FLYING SOLO 41

RAGE OVER A LOST PENNY 43

1. Above & Beyond

Moderately
Jennifer Eklund

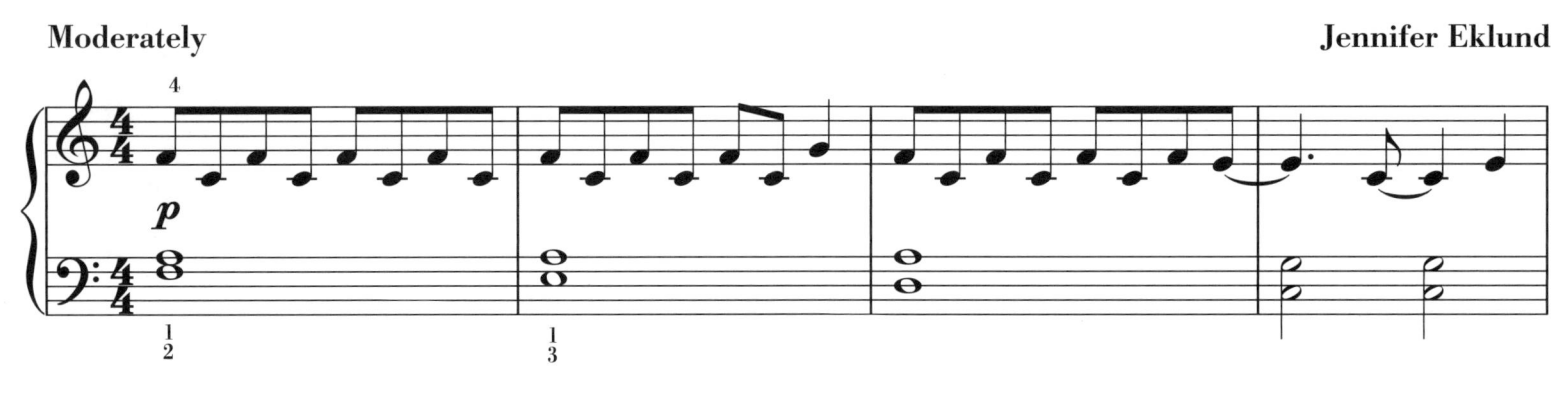
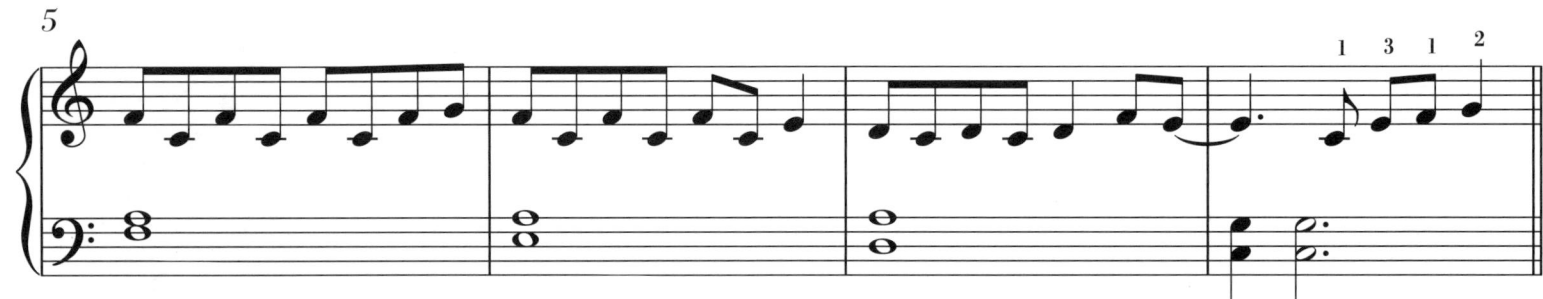

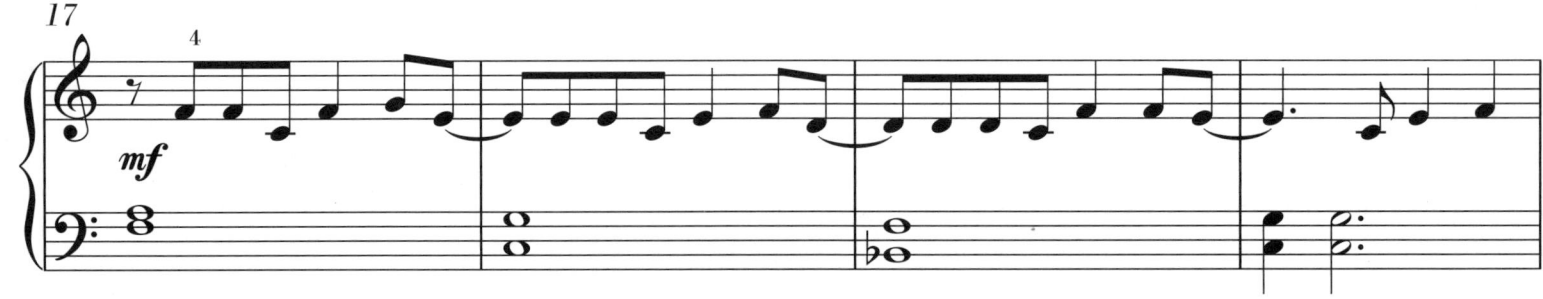

Copyright © 2013 Piano Pronto Publishing, Inc.
All Rights Reserved | PianoPronto.com

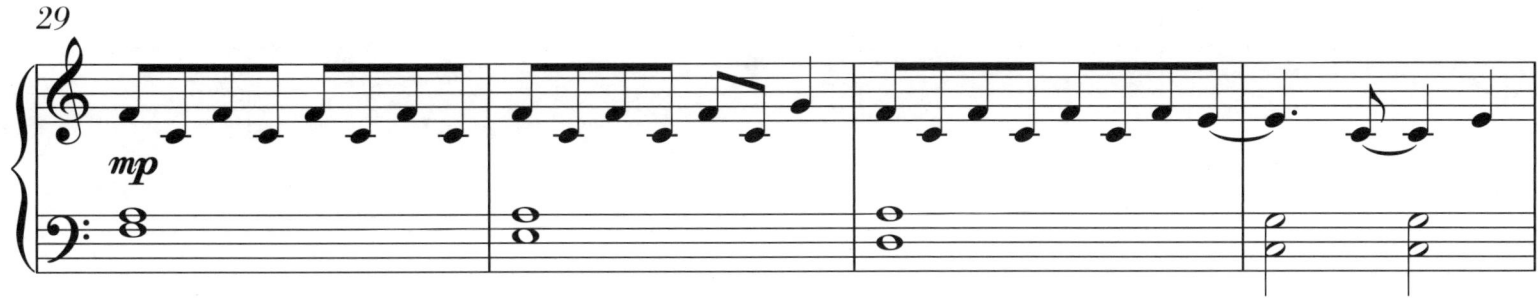

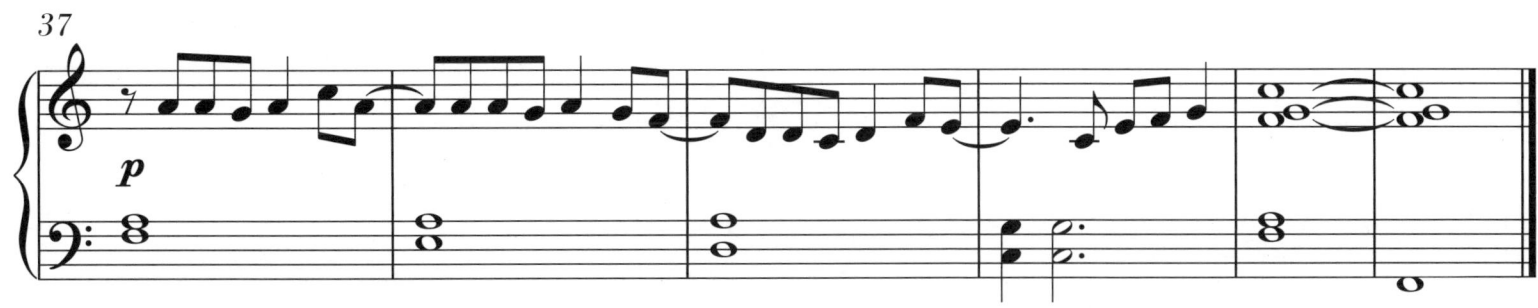

2. The Stars & Stripes Forever

John Philip Sousa
Arr. Jennifer Eklund

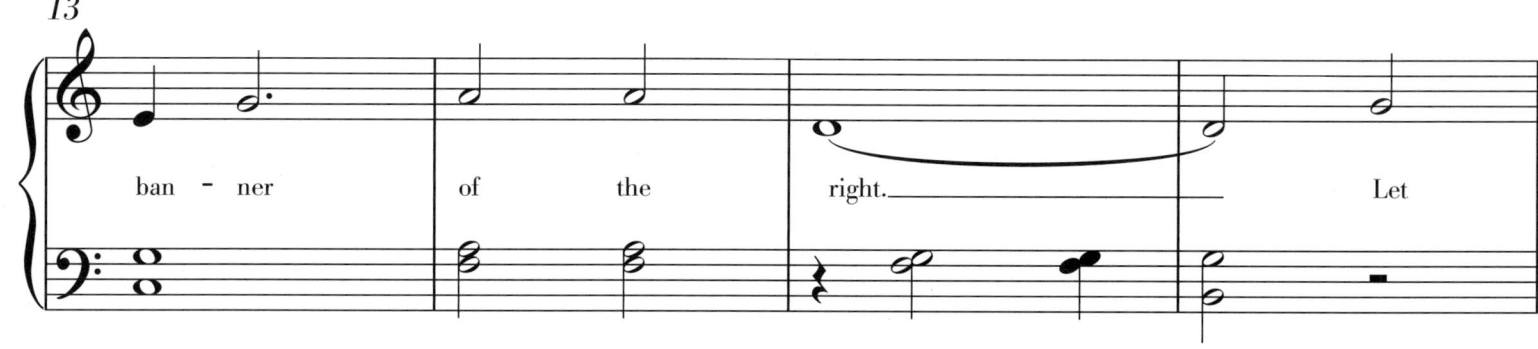

Copyright © 2013 Piano Pronto Publishing, Inc.
All Rights Reserved | PianoPronto.com

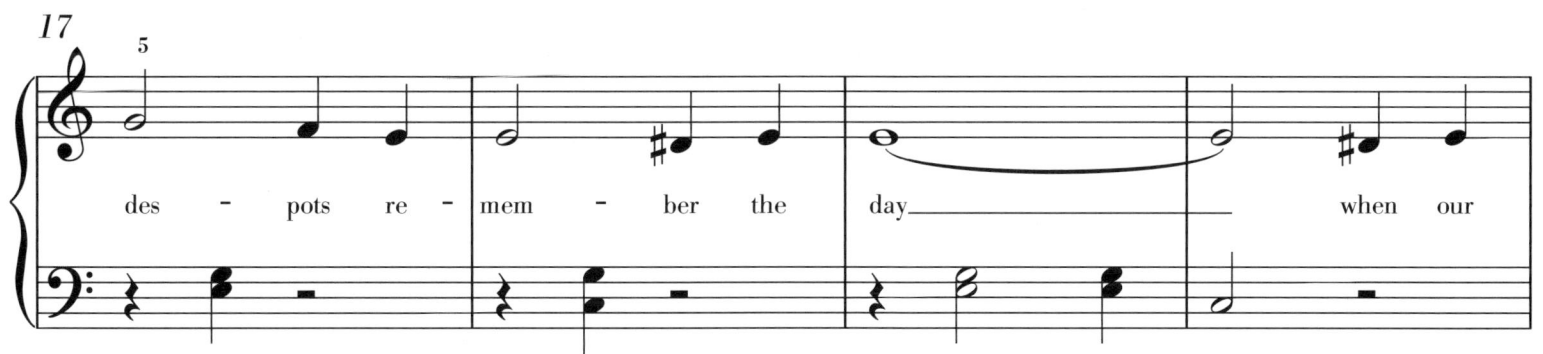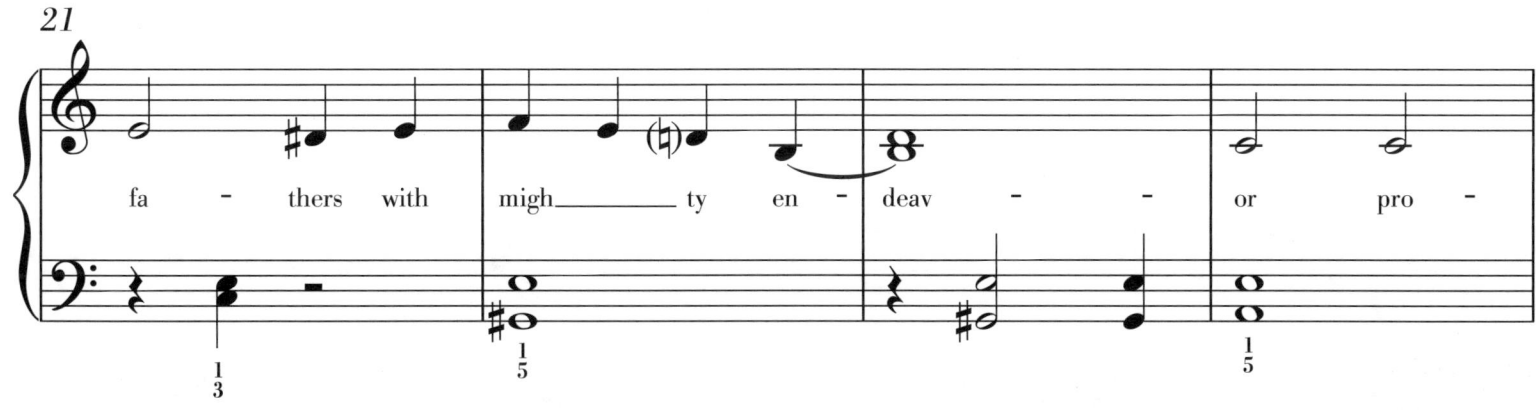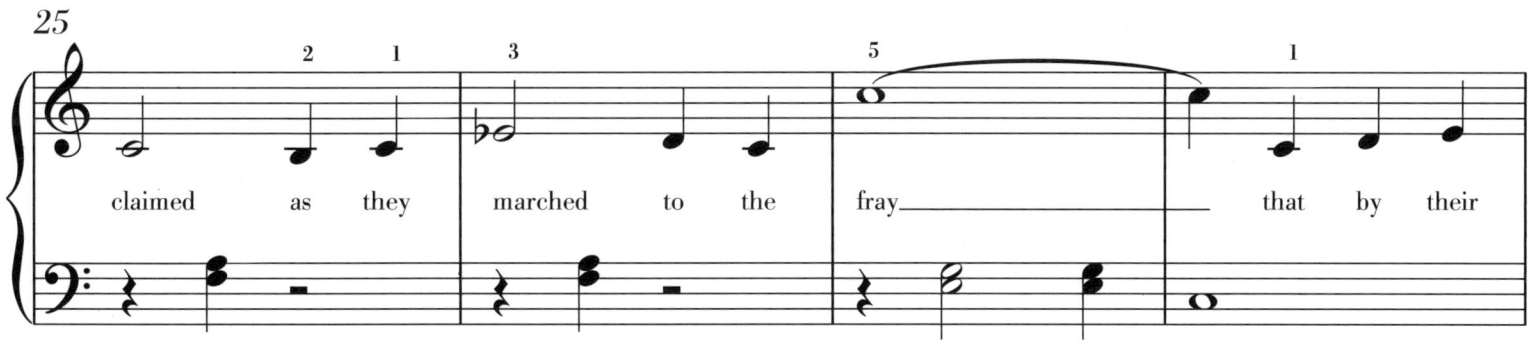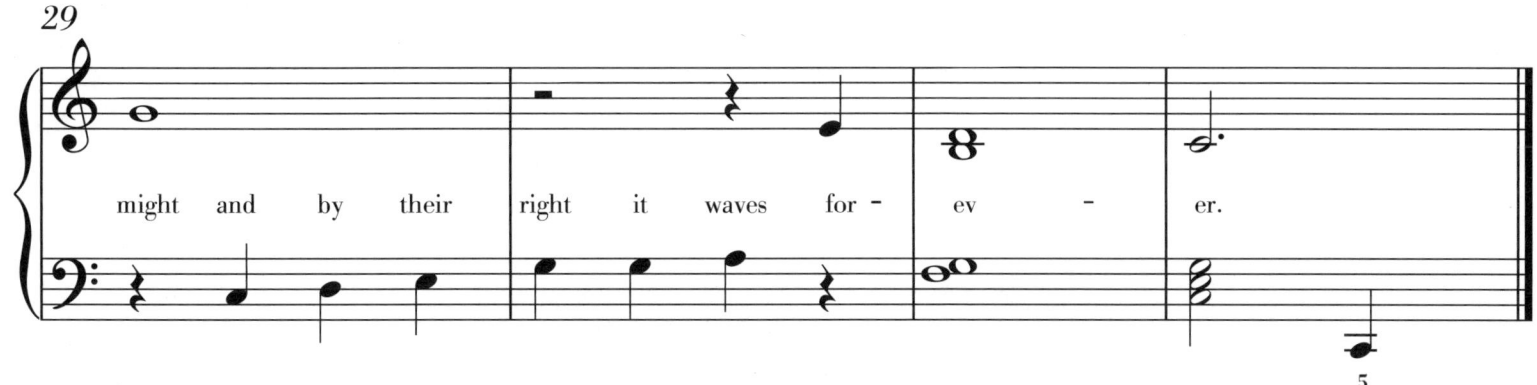

3. In the Hall of the Mountain King

Edvard Grieg
Arr. Jennifer Eklund

Mysteriously

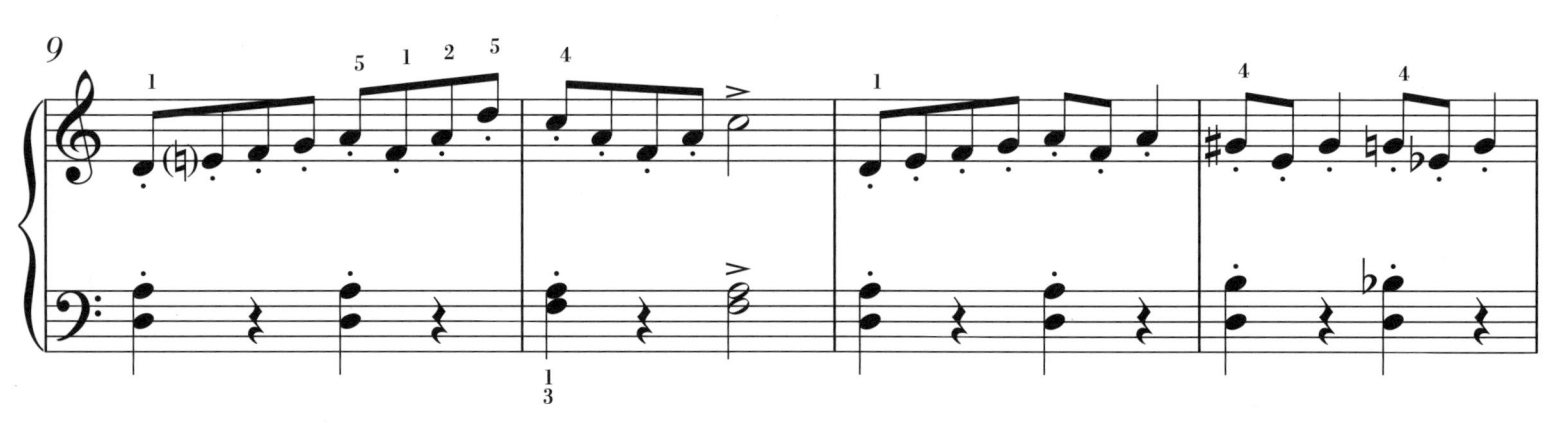

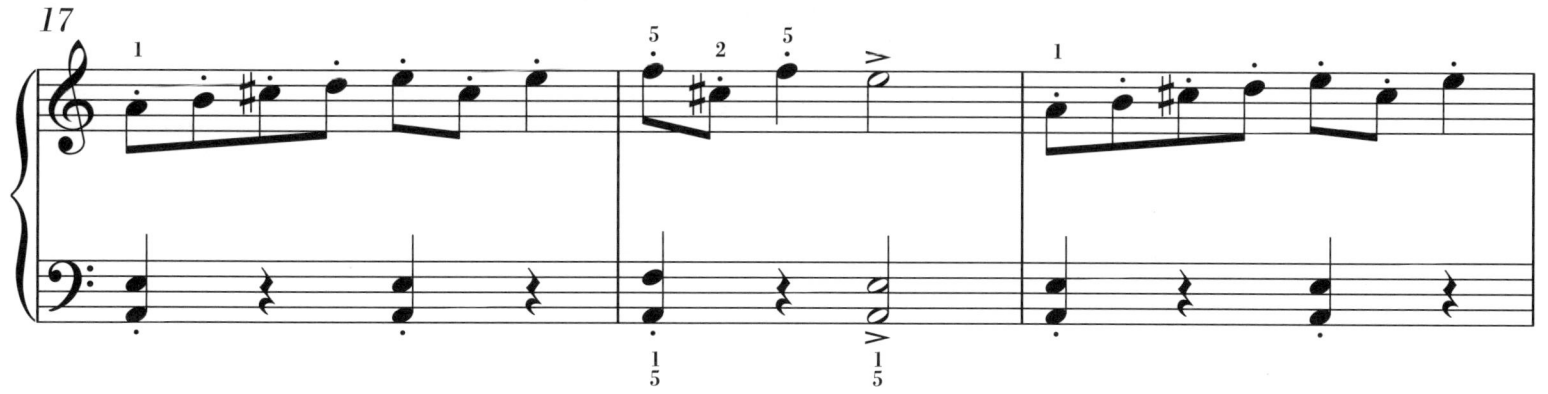

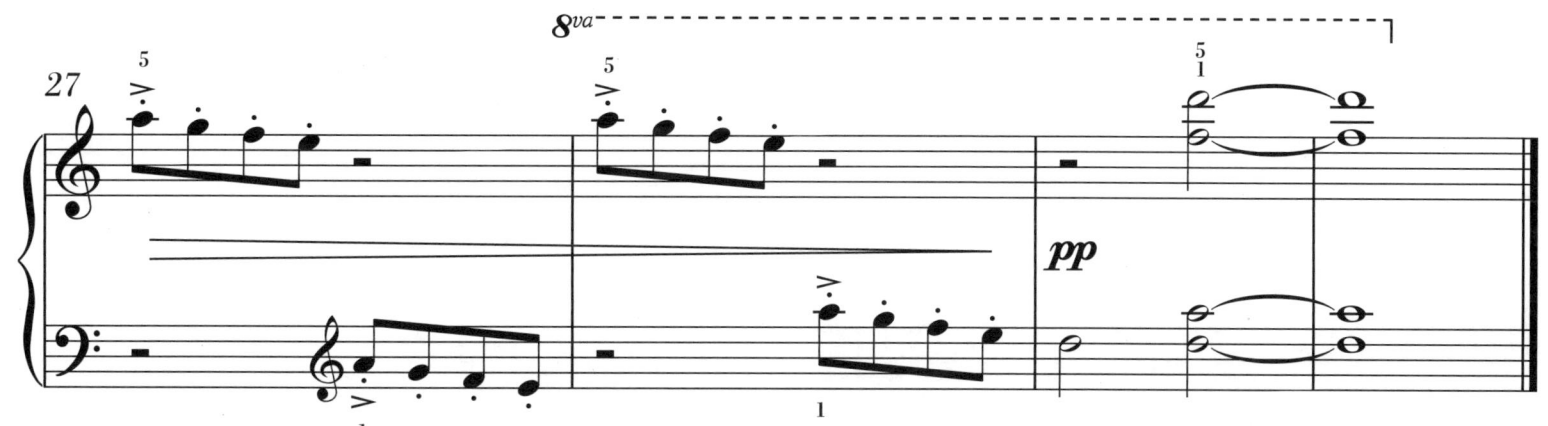

4. You're a Grand Old Flag

George M. Cohan
Arr. Jennifer Eklund

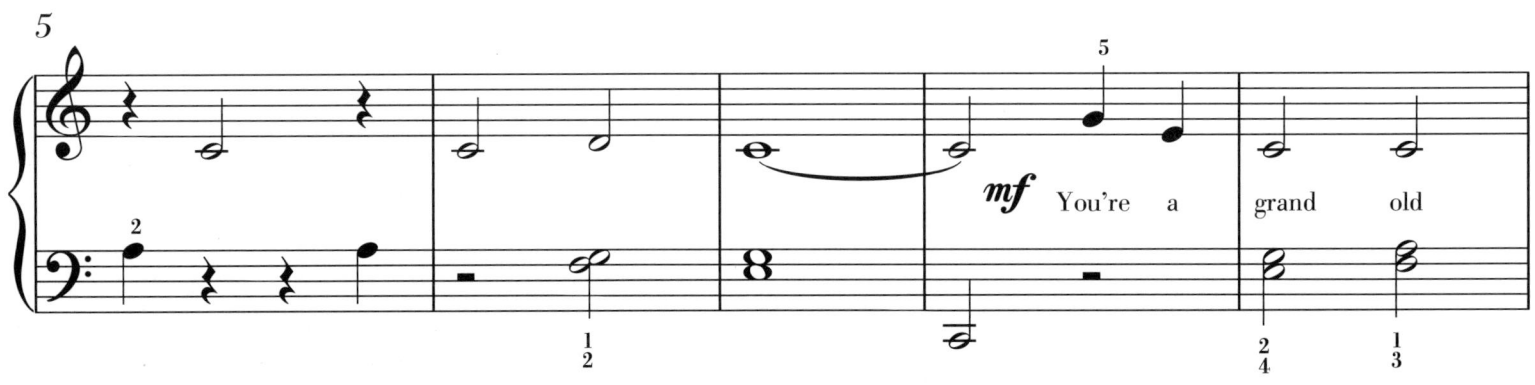
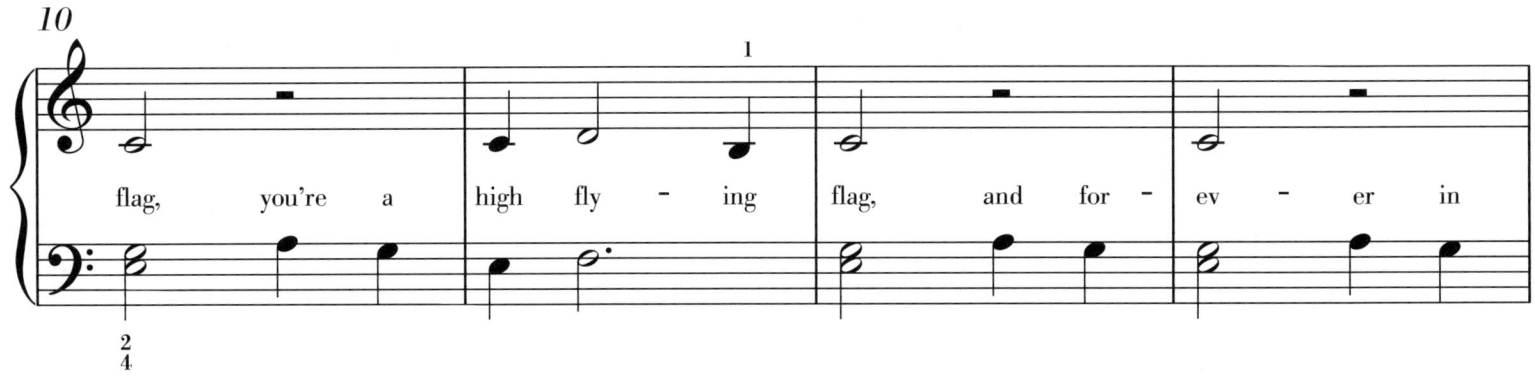

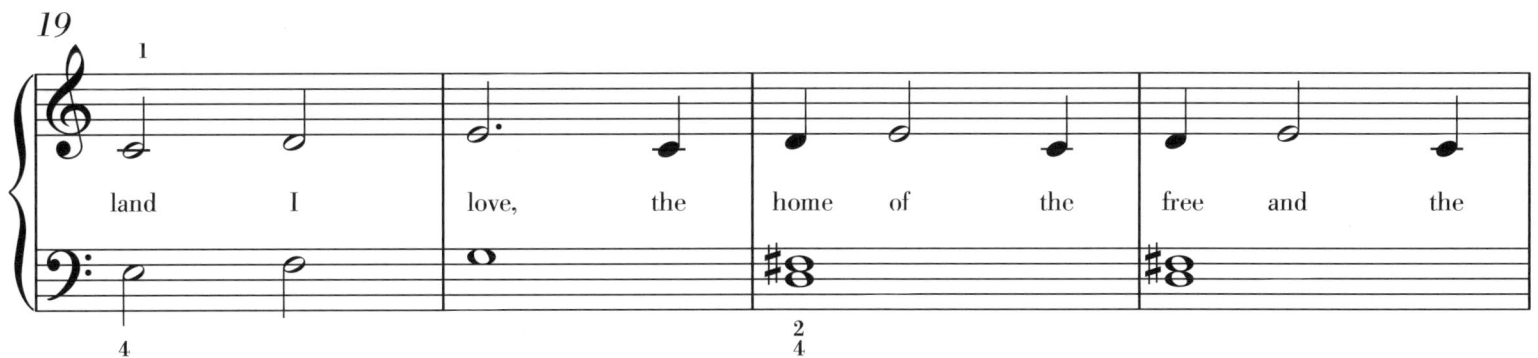
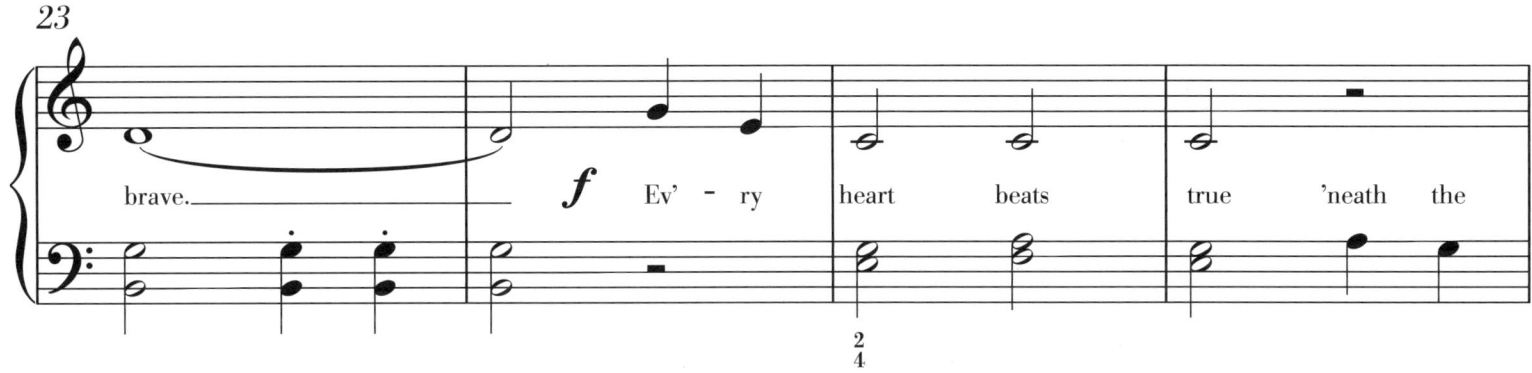

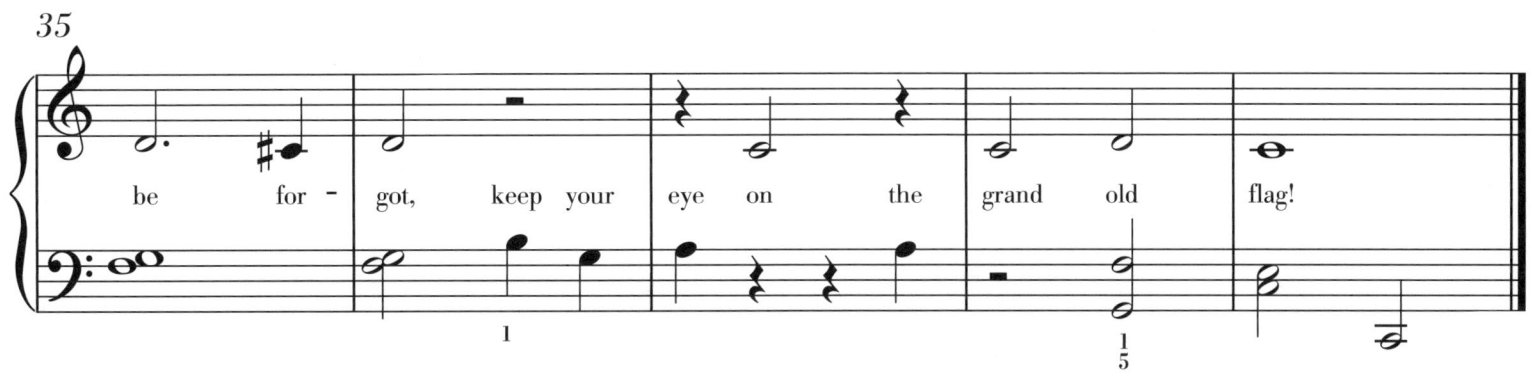

5. Rondalla Aragonesa

Enrique Granados
Arr. Jennifer Eklund

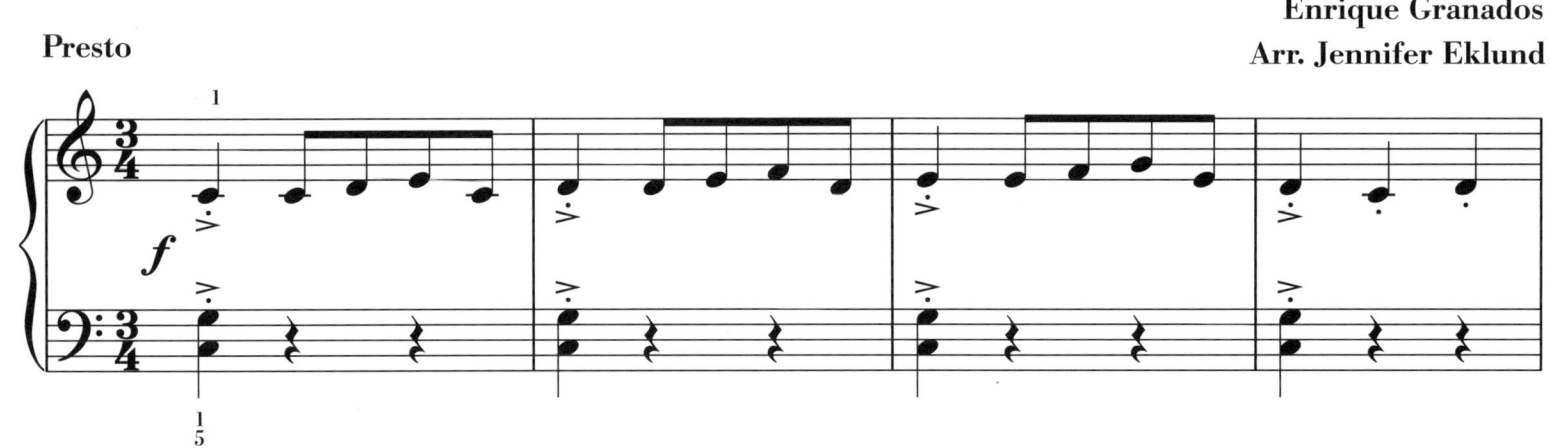

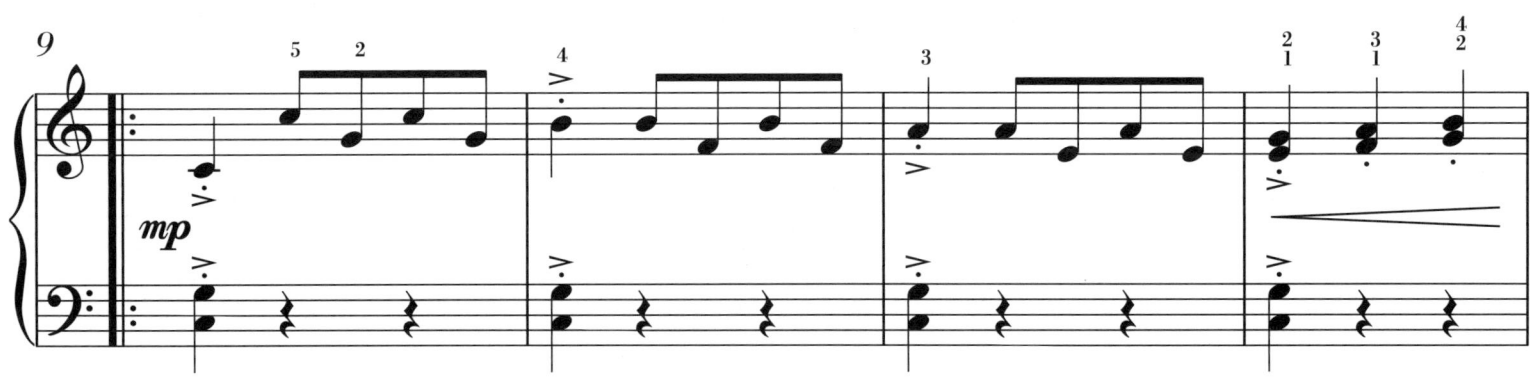

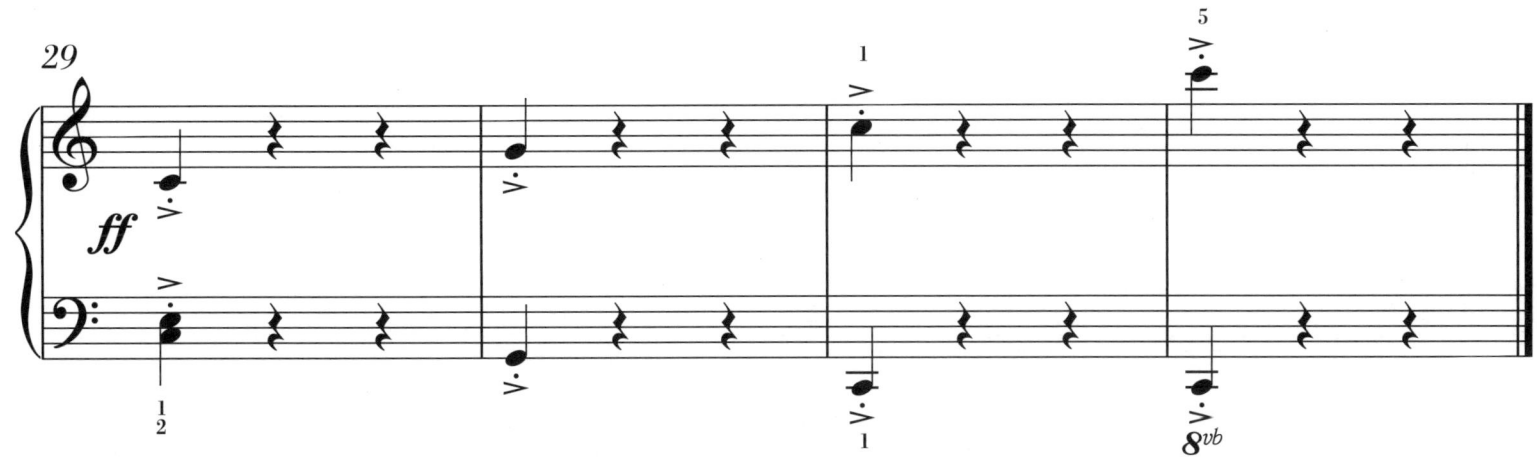

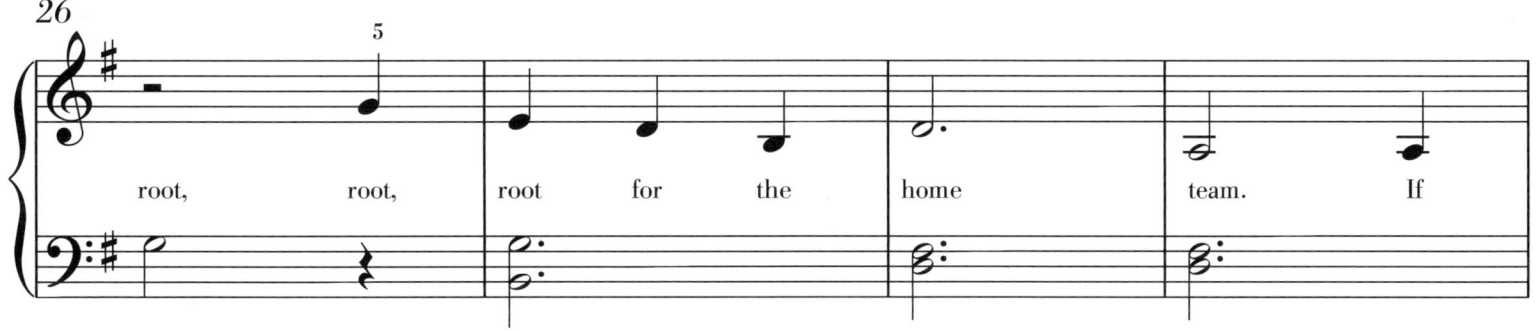
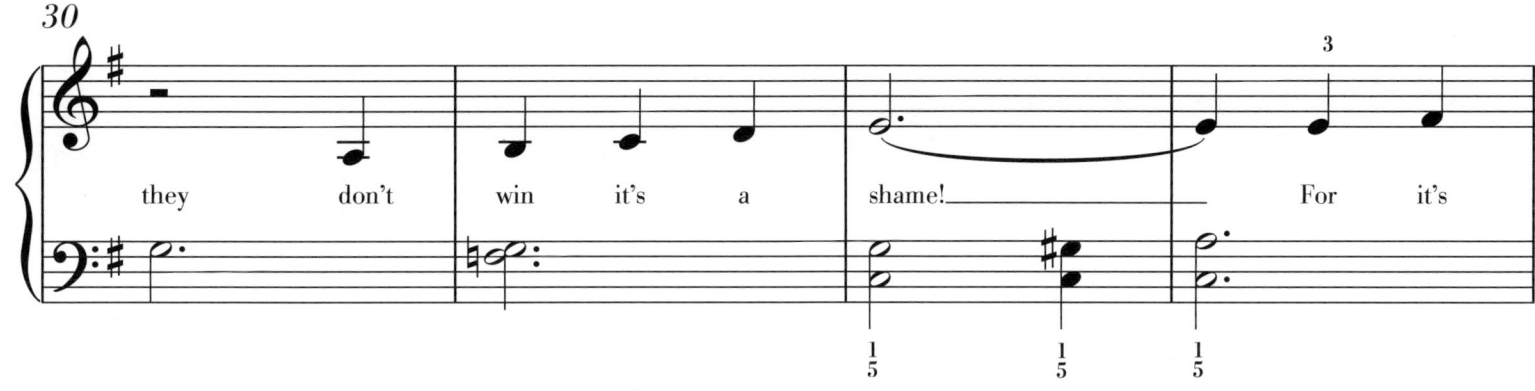

7. Canon

Johann Pachelbel
Arr. Jennifer Eklund

Andante

8. Hungarian Rhapsody

Franz Liszt
Arr. Jennifer Eklund

Vivace

9. Je te veux

Erik Satie
Arr. Jennifer Eklund

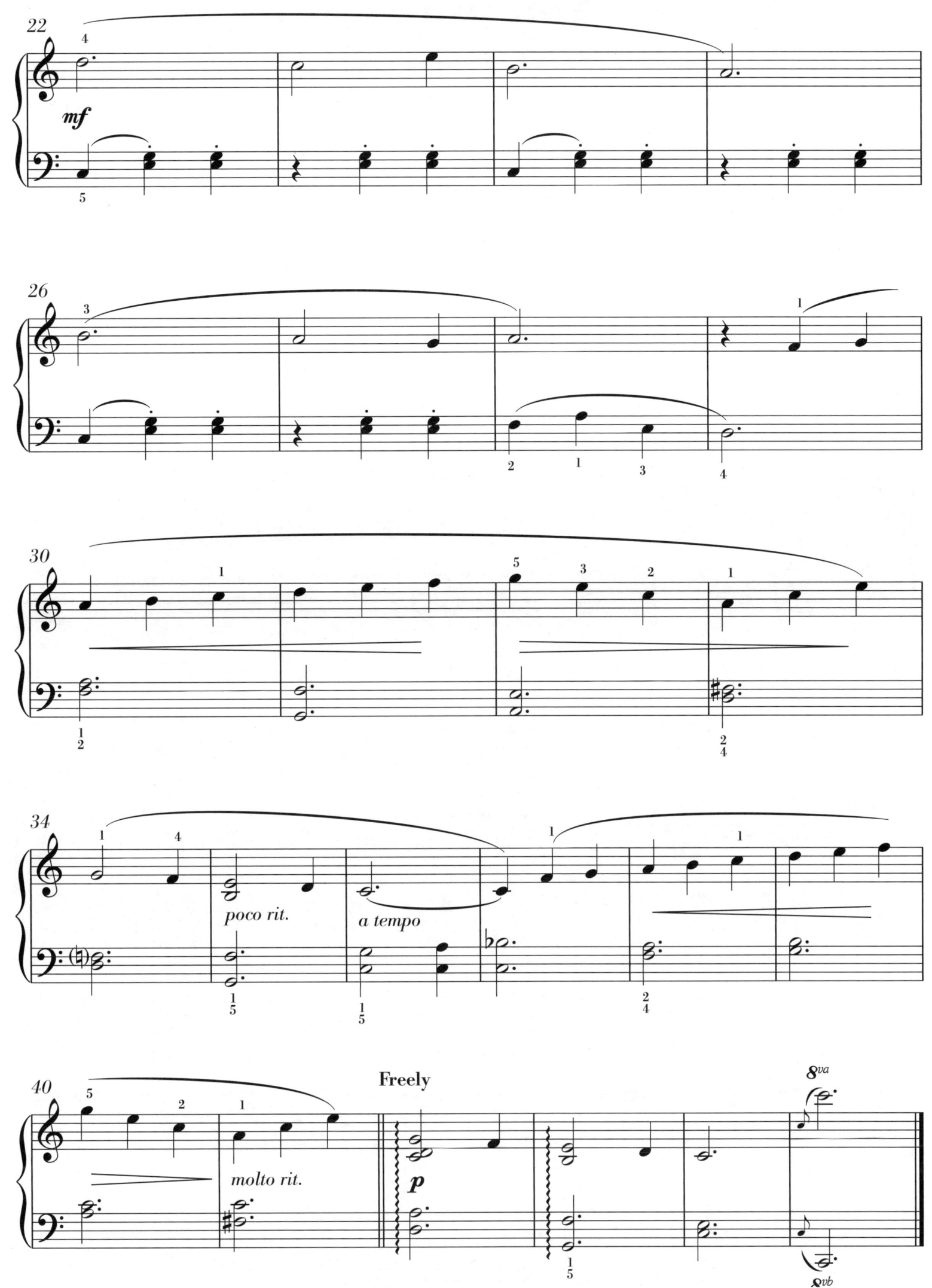

10. Non più andrai

W.A. Mozart
Arr. Jennifer Eklund

Allegro

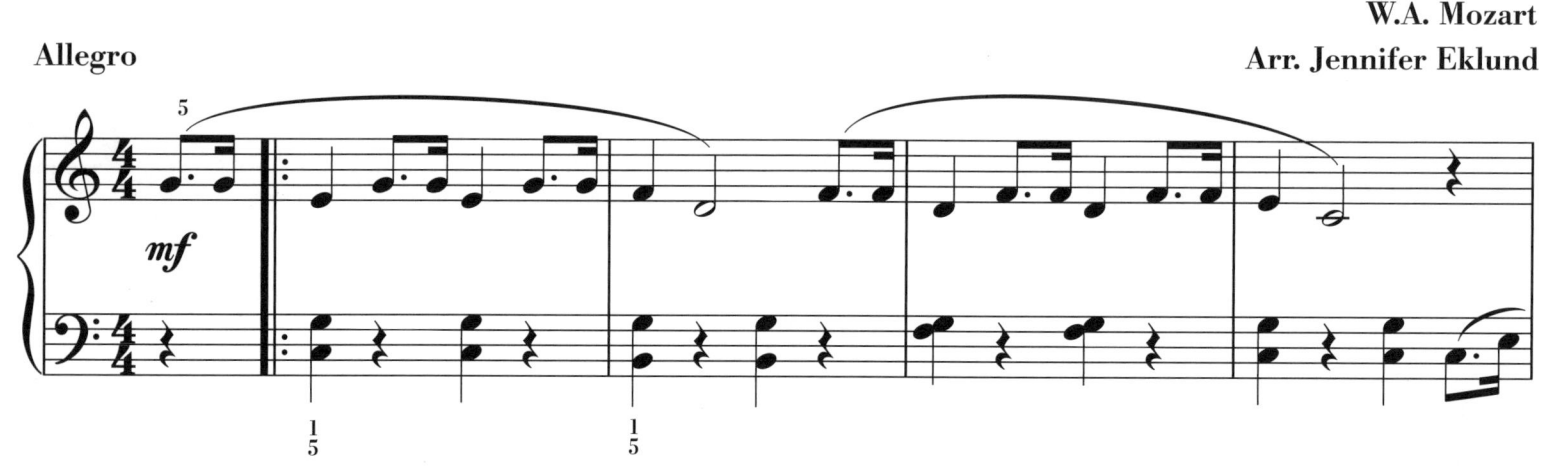
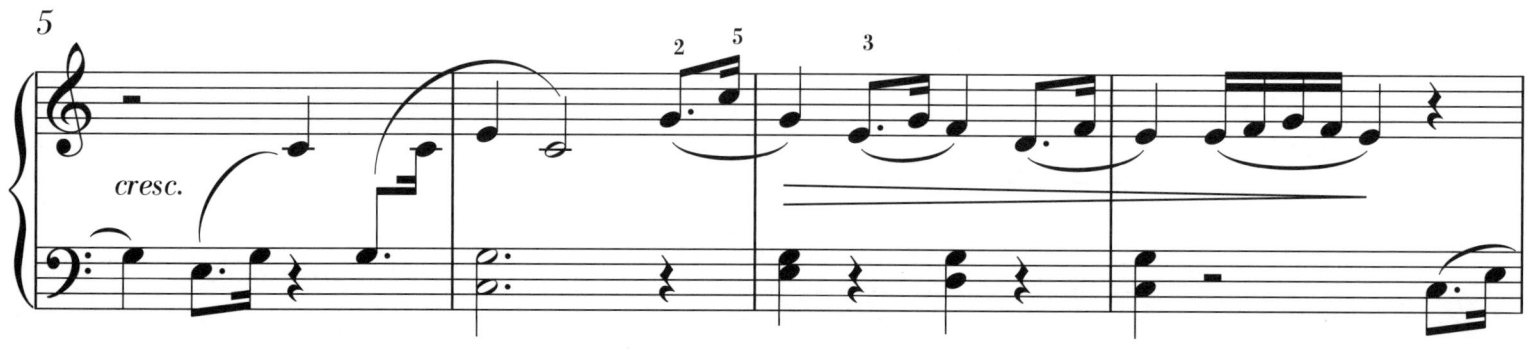

11. The Return

Jennifer Eklund

12. Pineapple Rag

Scott Joplin
Arr. Jennifer Eklund

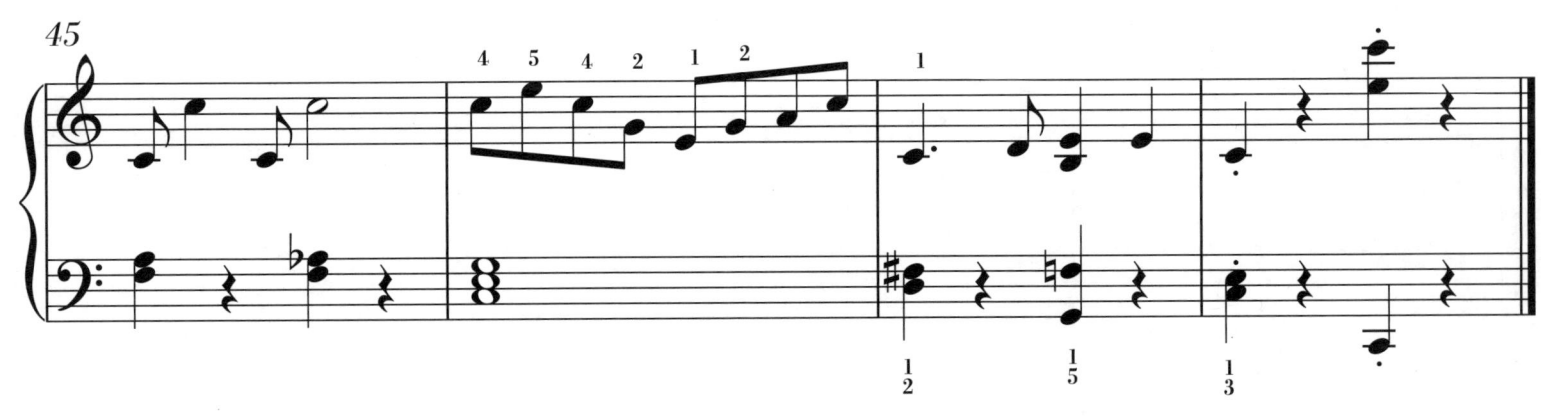

13. Whirlwind

Jennifer Eklund

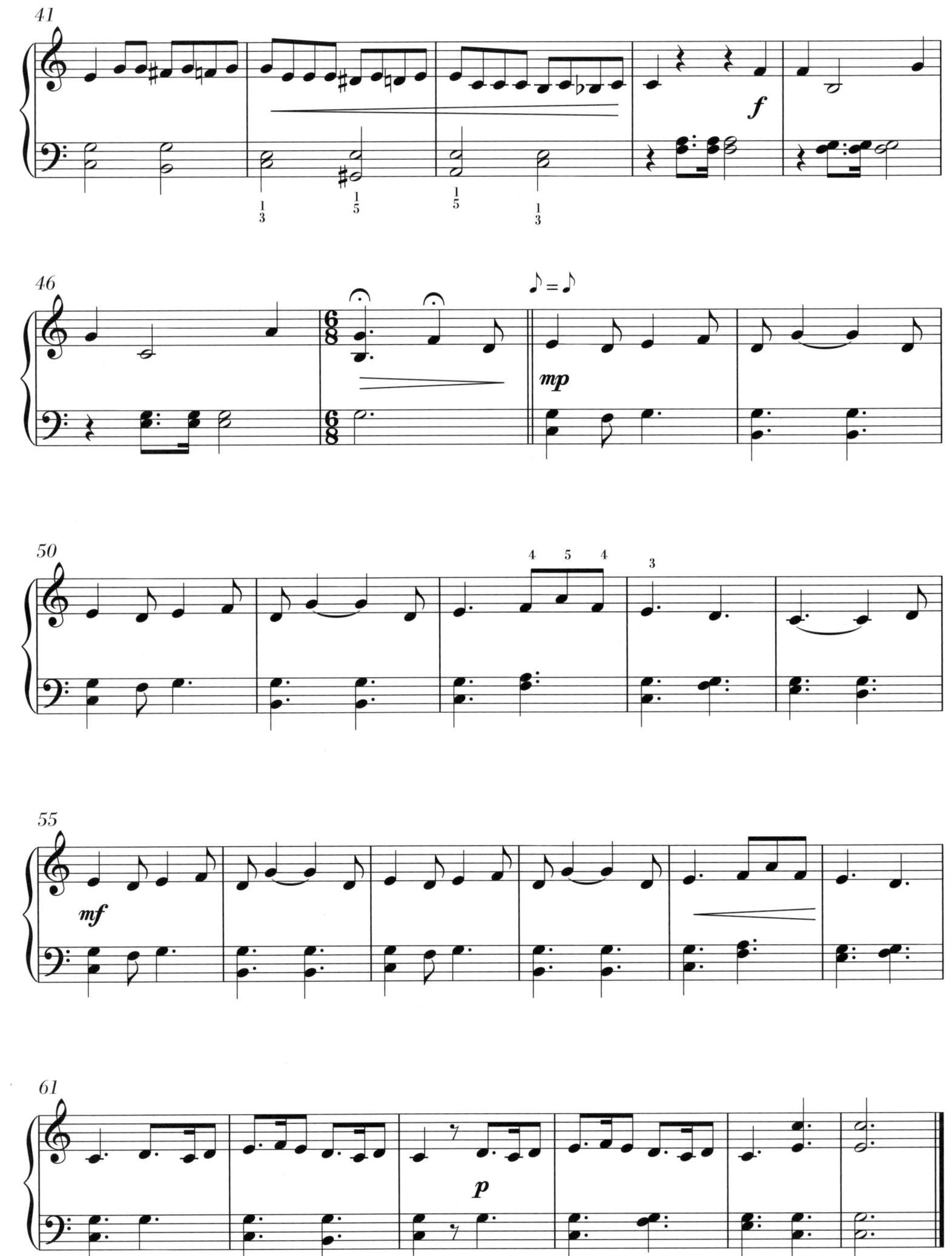

15. Turkish March

Ludwig van Beethoven
Arr. Jennifer Eklund

Giocoso

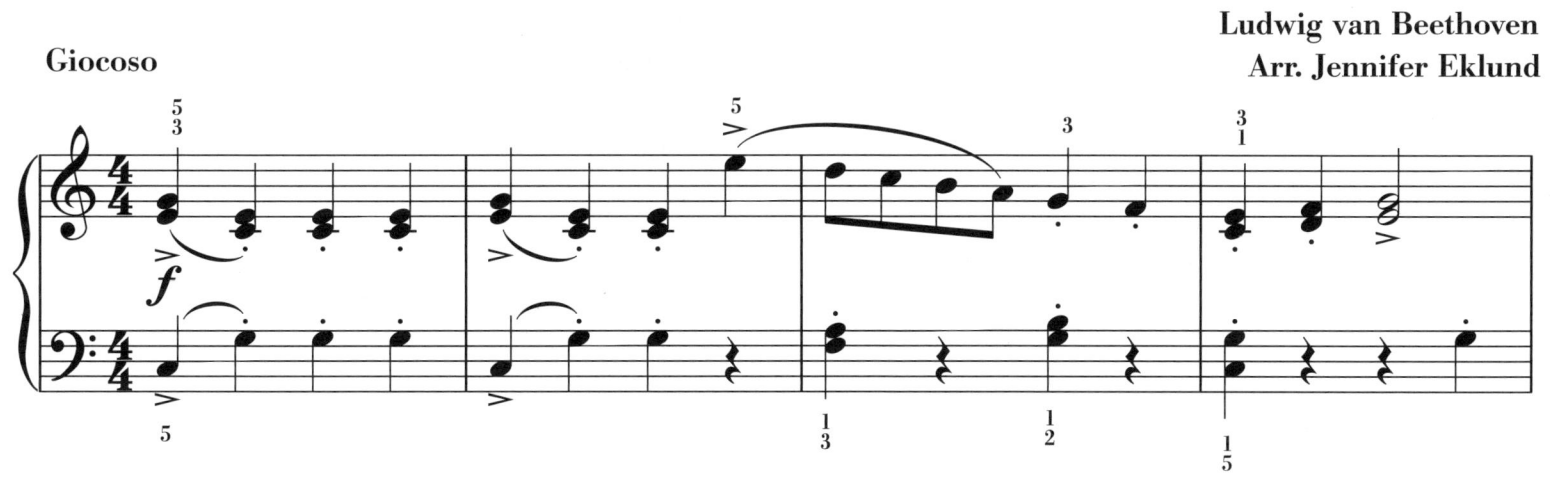
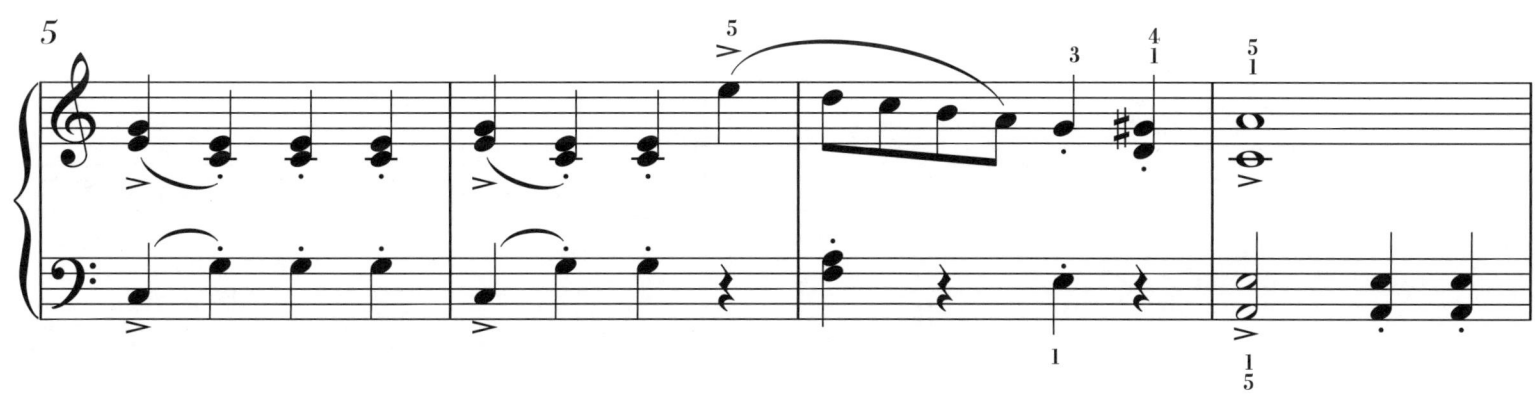

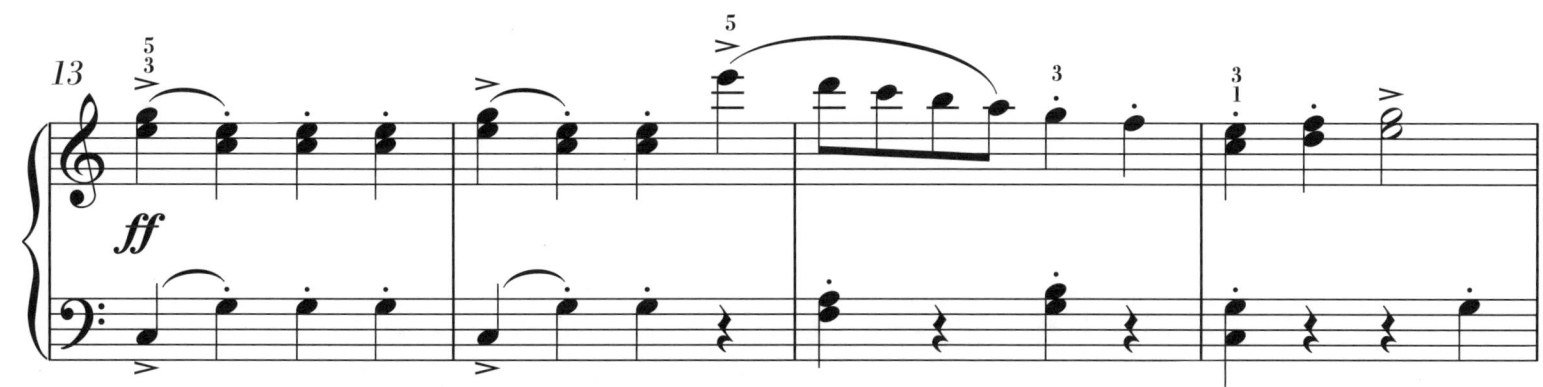

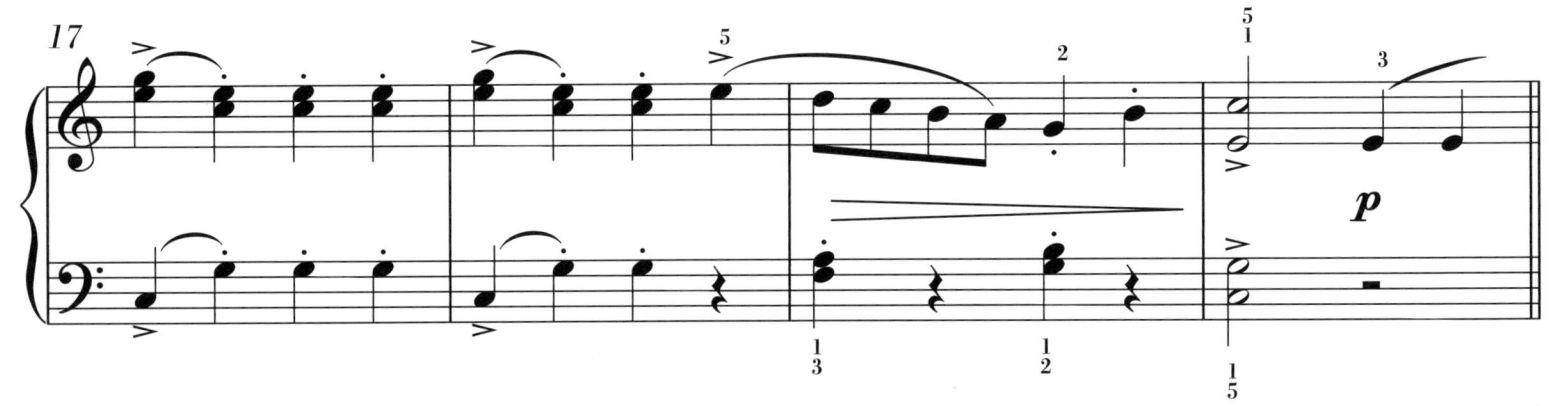
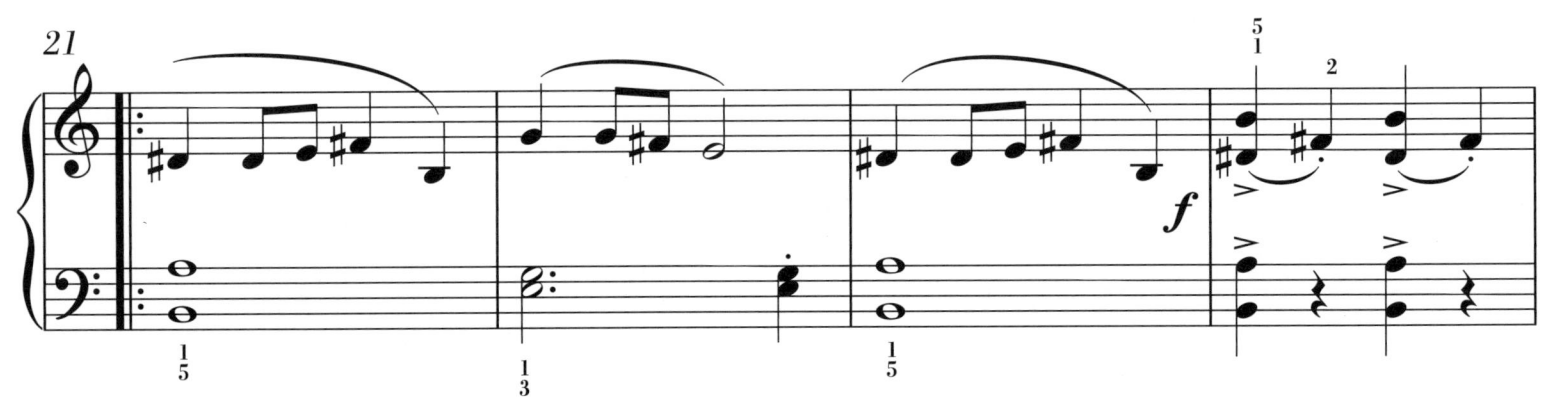

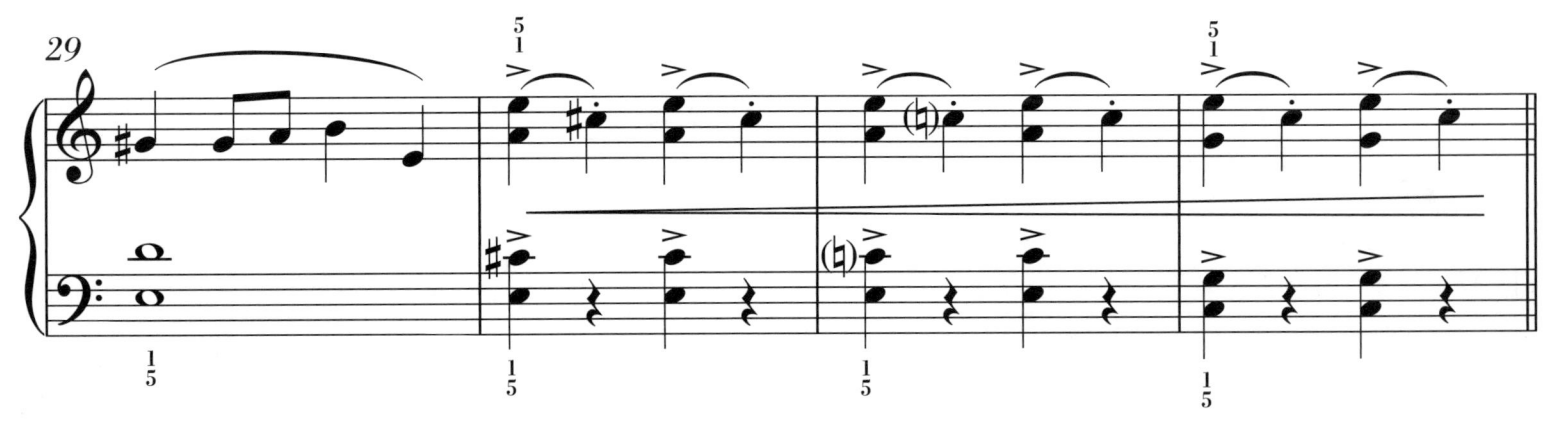

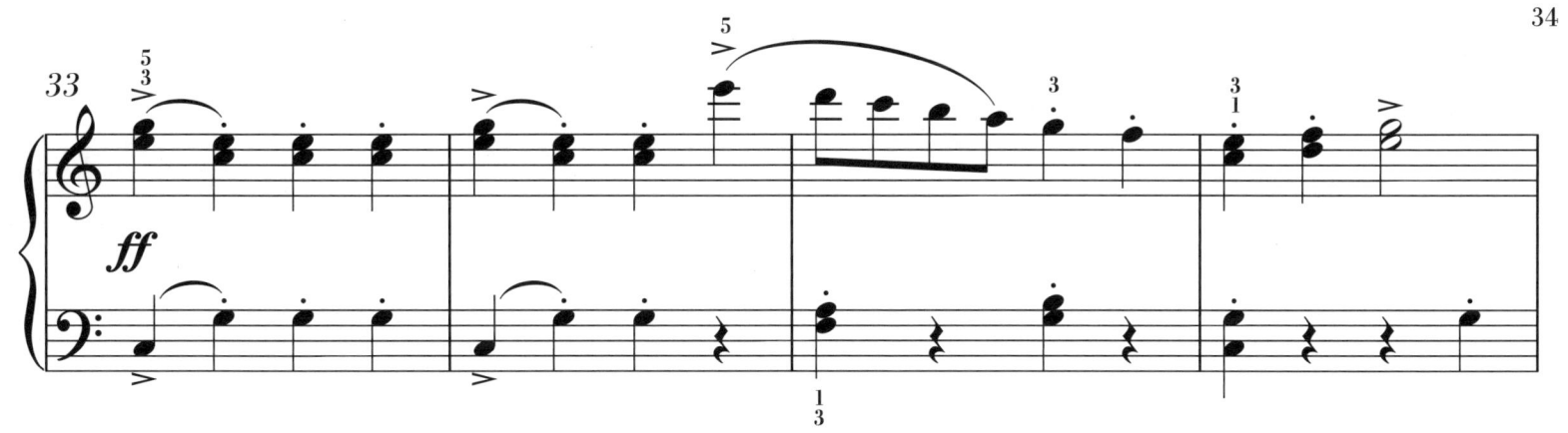
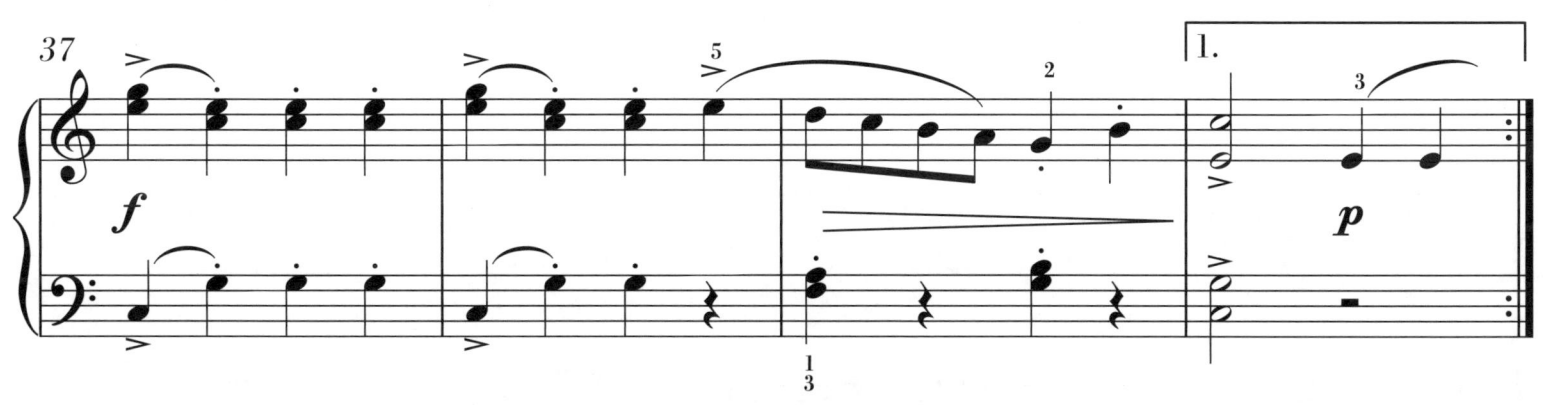

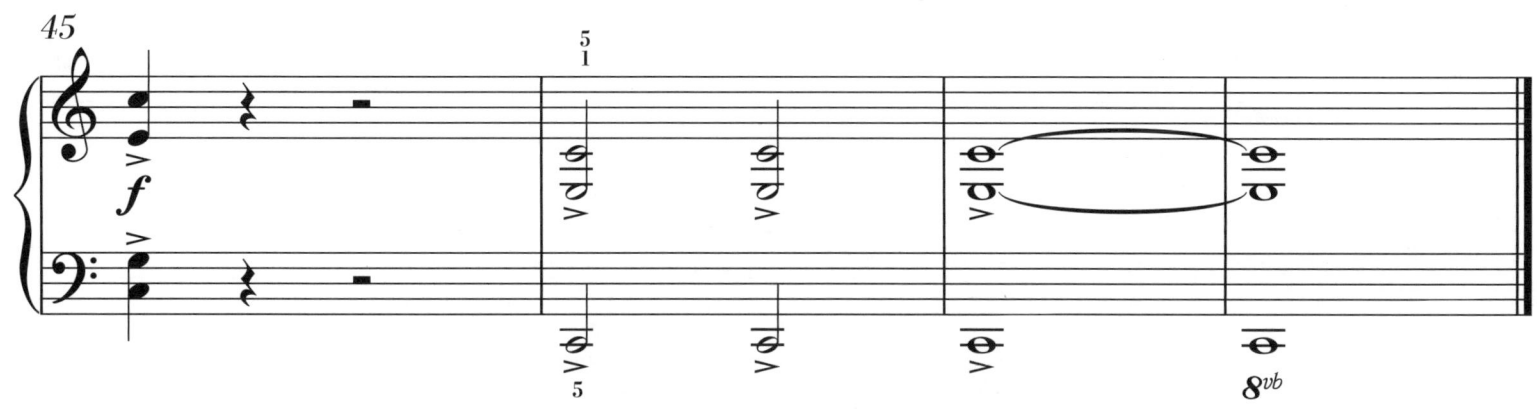

16. Maple Leaf Rag

Scott Joplin
Arr. Jennifer Eklund

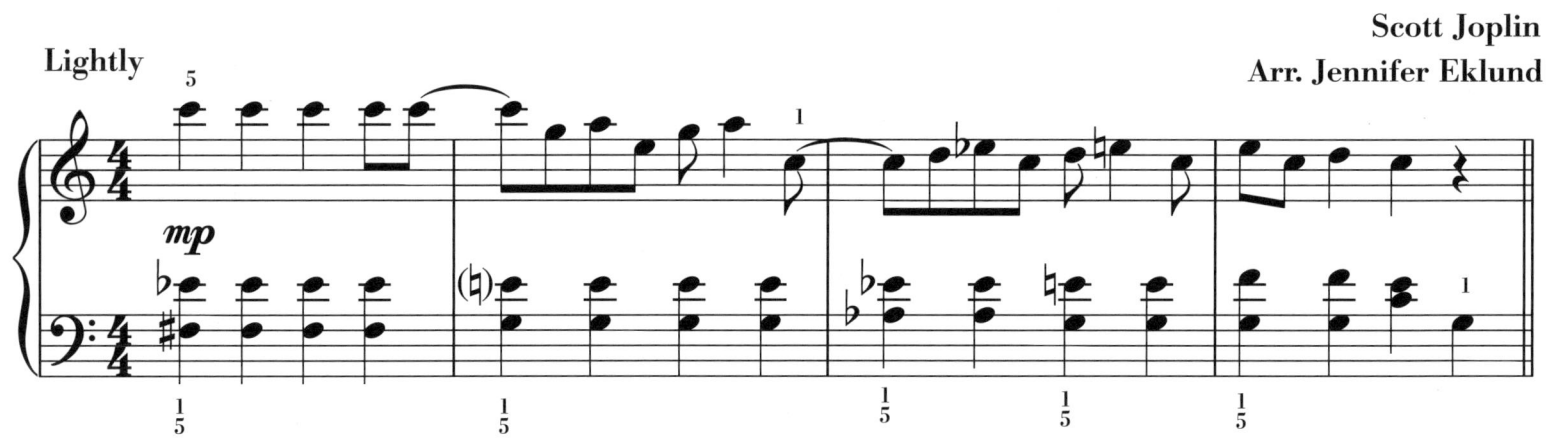

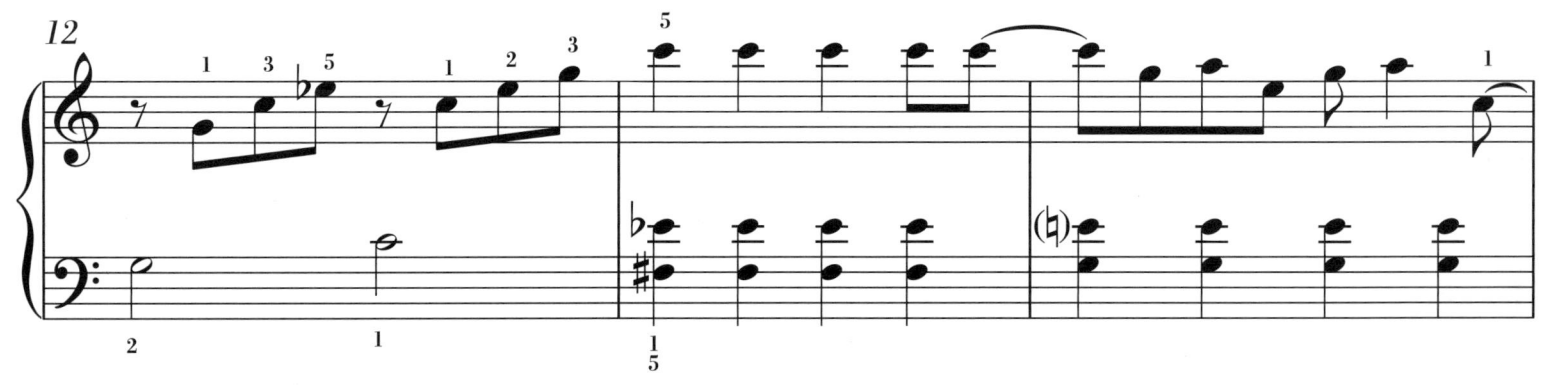

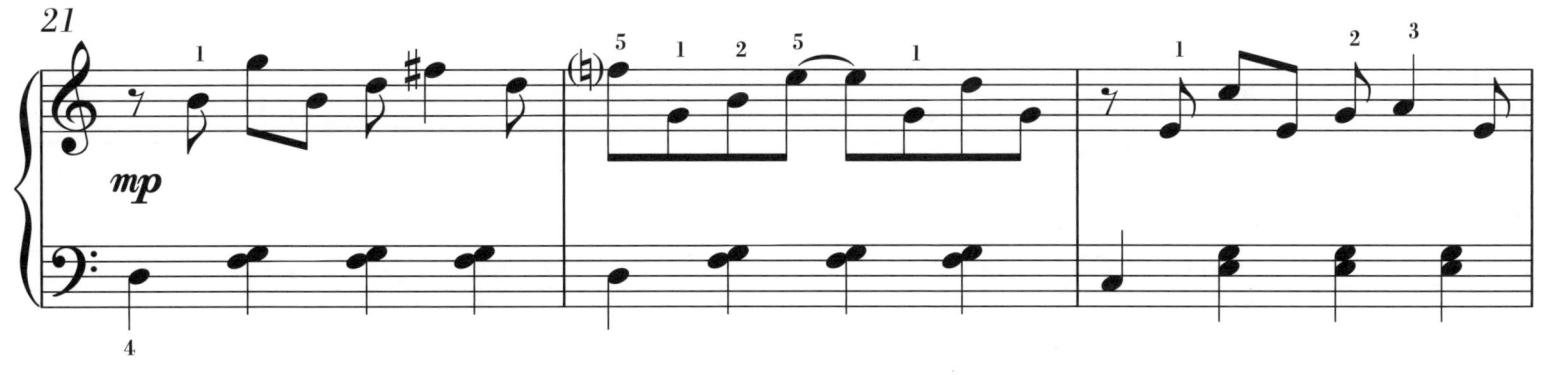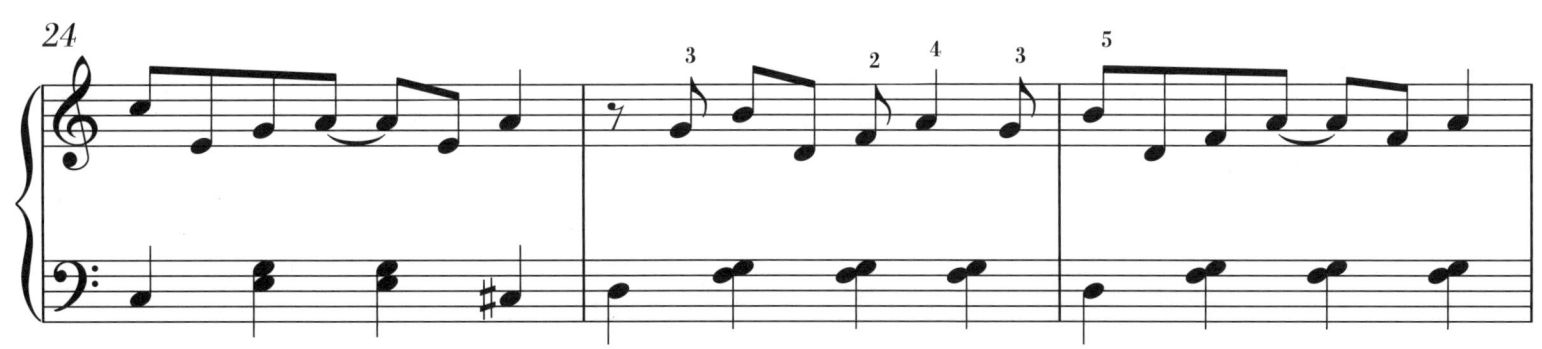

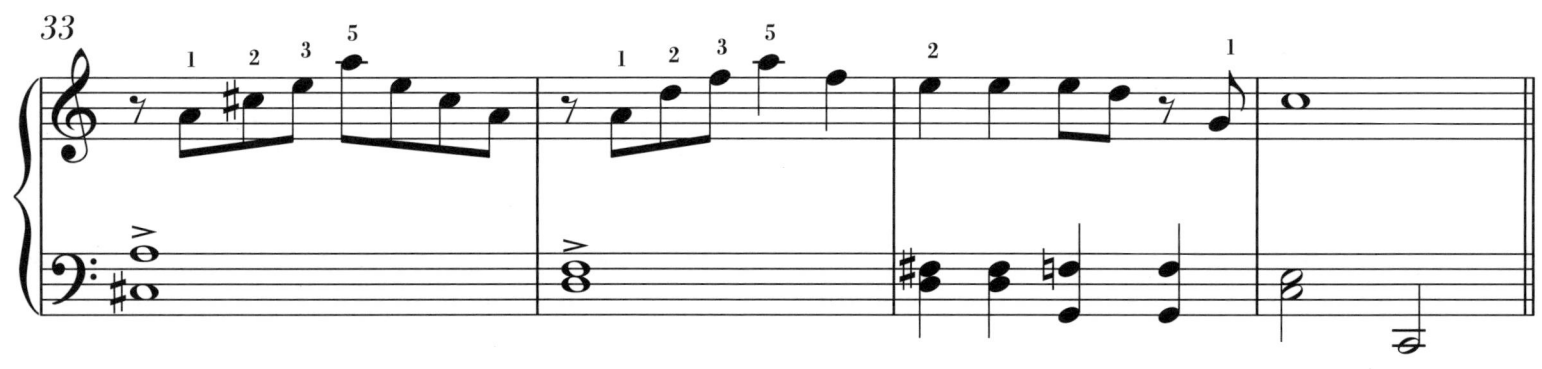
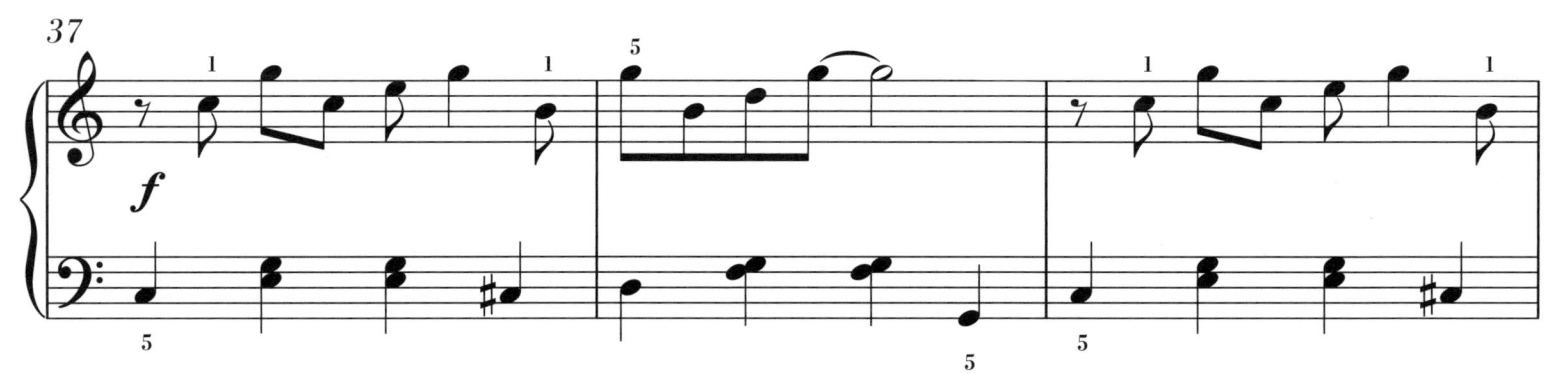

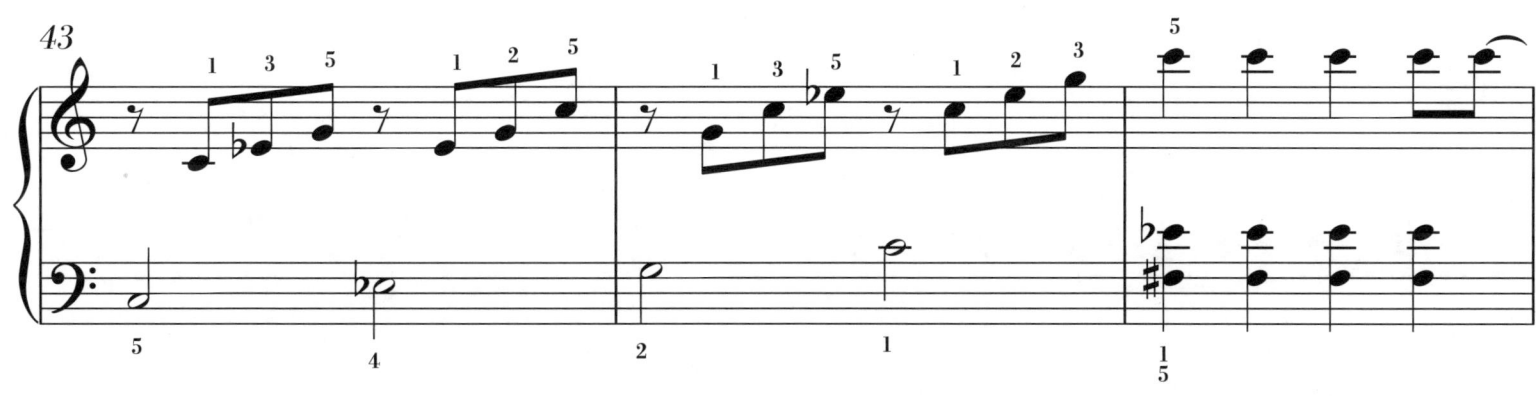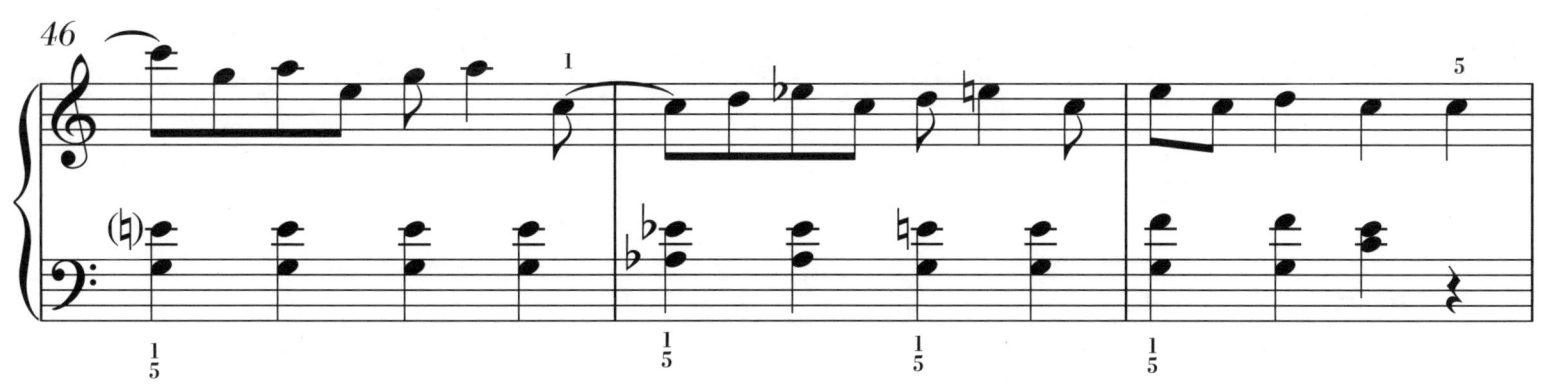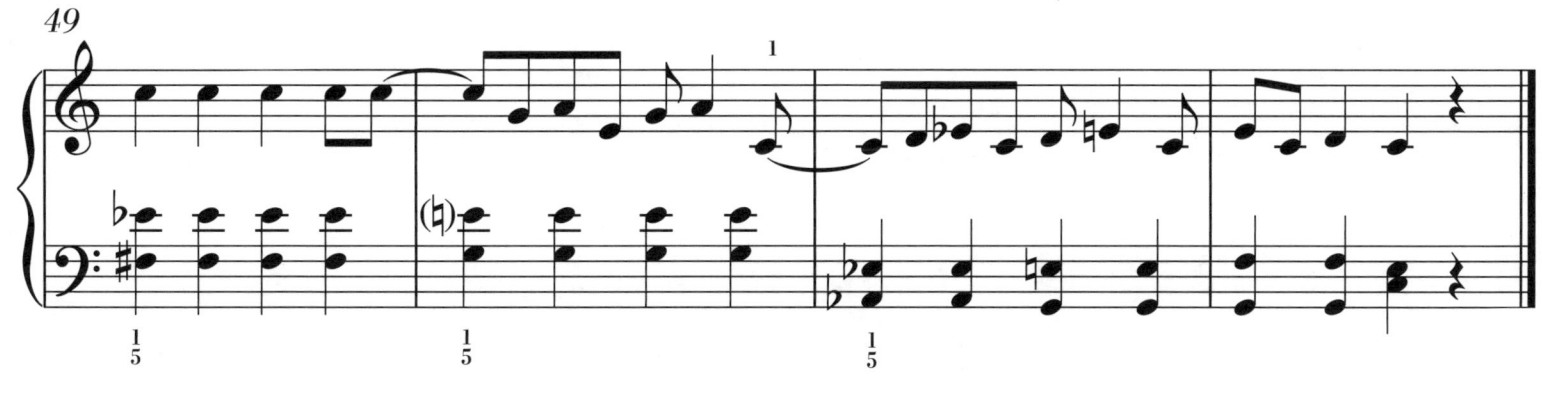

17. Thursday Blues

Jennifer Eklund

18. Flying Solo

Jennifer Eklund

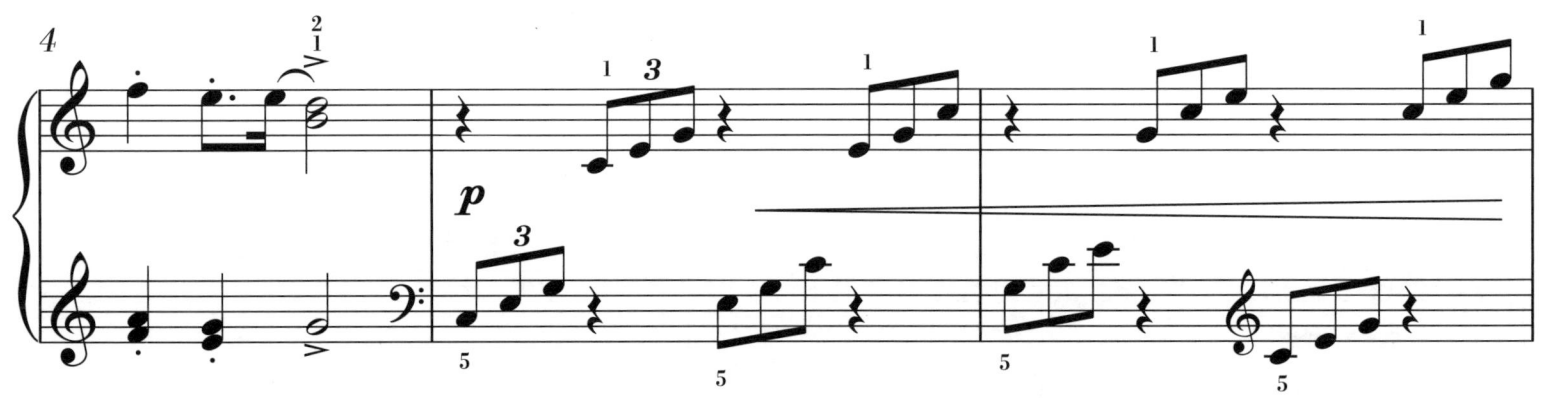

19. Rage over a Lost Penny

Ludwig van Beethoven
Arr. Jennifer Eklund

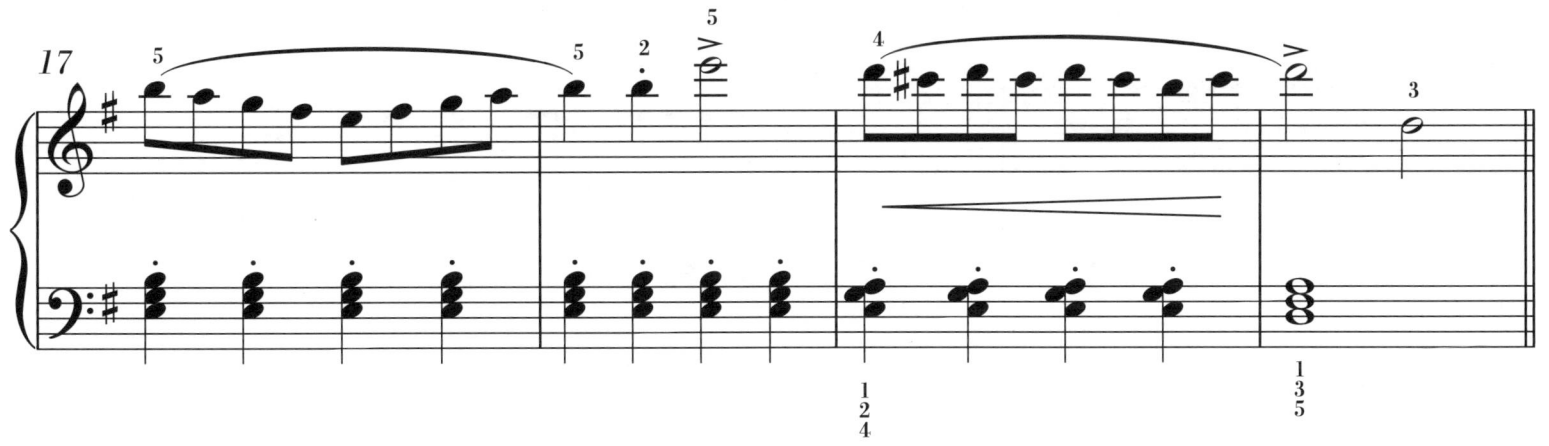
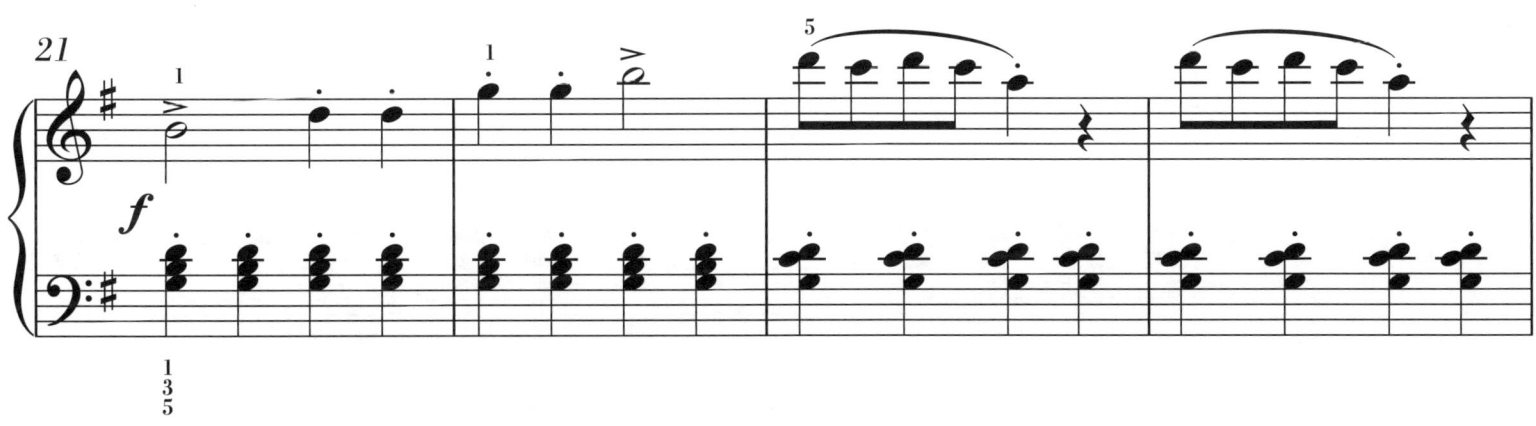
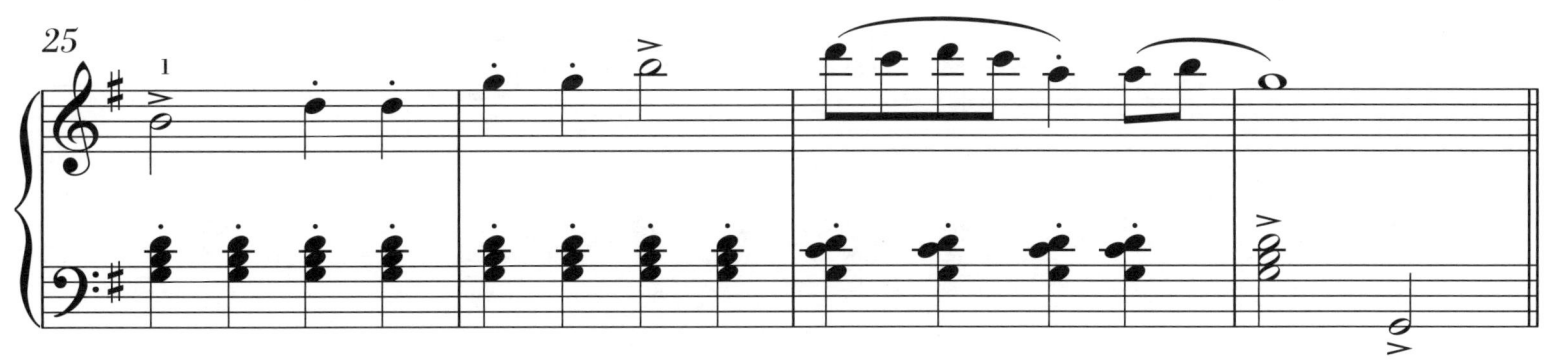
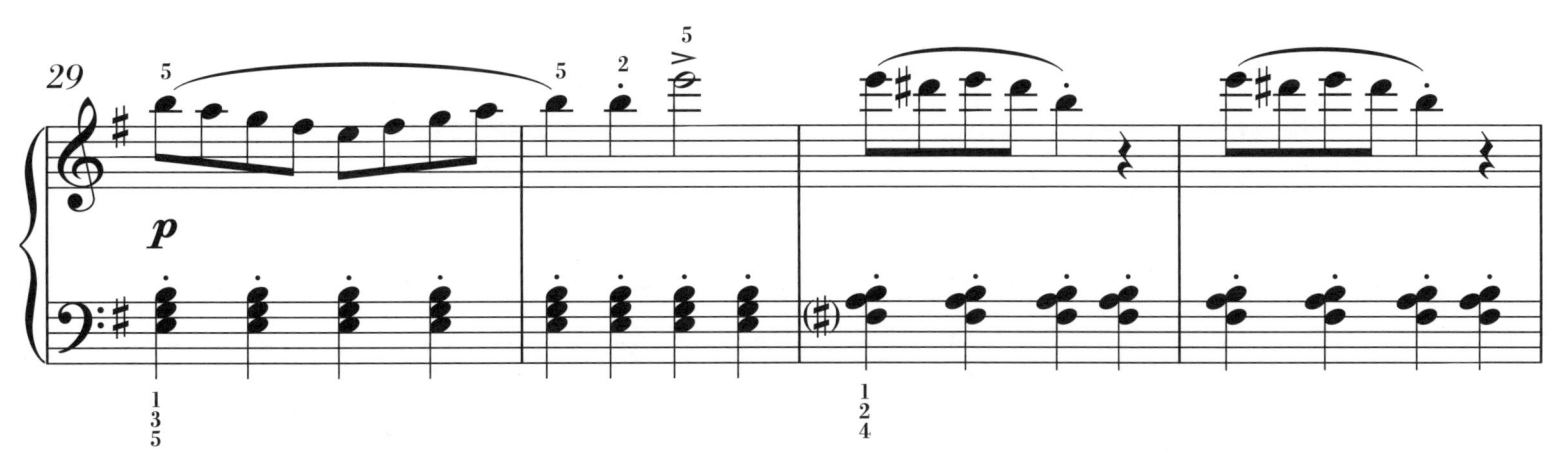

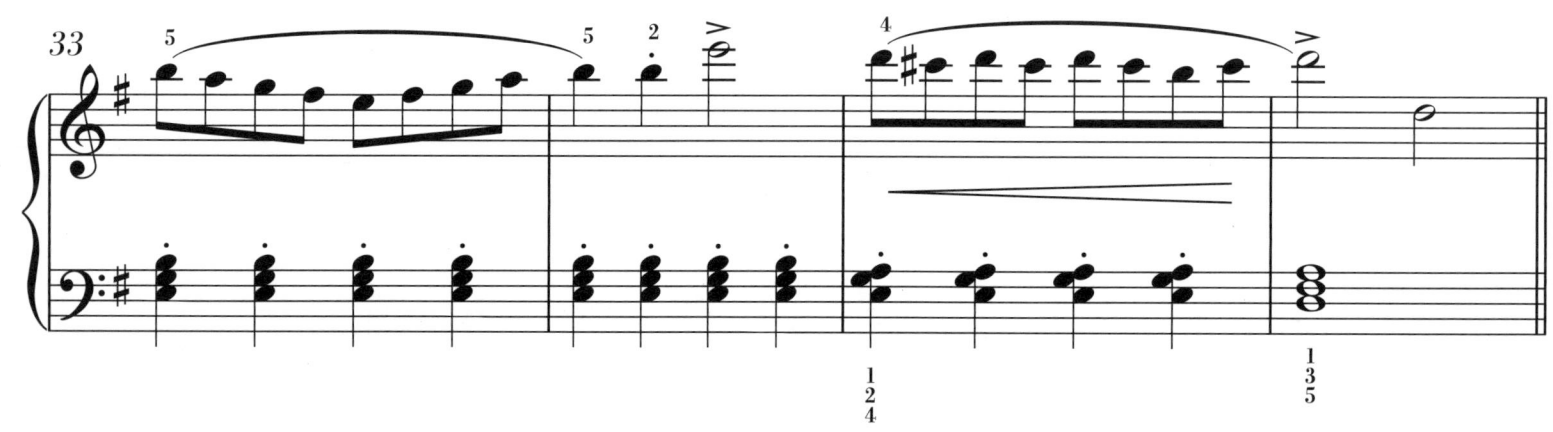

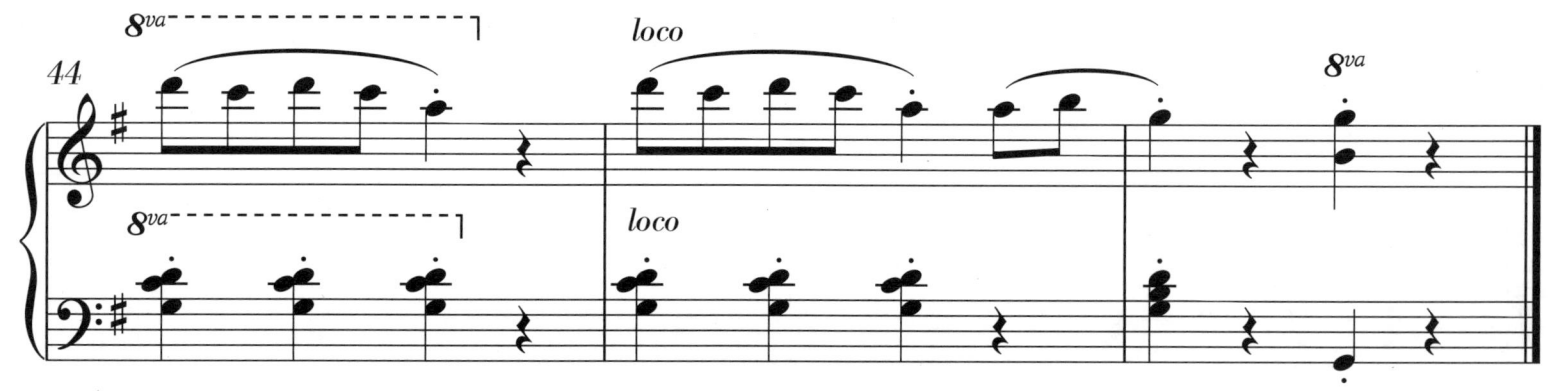